Reflections Revisited

Reflections Revisited

A Collection of Poetry and 3 Wicked Excellent Short Stories

Written and Illustrated by
Norma Jean Campanaro

Copyright © 2023 **Norma Jean Campanaro Publishing**

All rights reserved. No part of this publication may be reproduced, distributed, or transmitted in any form or by any means, including photocopying, recording, or other electronic or mechanical methods, without the prior written permission of the publisher, except in the case of brief quotations embodied in critical reviews and certain other noncommercial uses permitted by copyright law. For permission requests, write to the publisher, addressed "Attention: Book Rights and Permission," at the address below.

Published in the United States of America

ISBN 978-1-955243-43-8 (SC)

Norma Jean Campanaro Publishing
222 West 6th Street
Suite 400, San Pedro, CA, 90731
www.stellarliterary.com

Order Information and Rights Permission:

Quantity sales. Special discounts might be available on quantity purchases by corporations, associations, and others. For details, contact the publisher at the address above.

For Book Rights Adaptation and other Rights Permission. Call us at toll-free 1-888-945-8513 or send us an email at admin@stellarliterary.com.

Contents

Raindrops 9
Think Again 10
Earth Realm 11
Imagine 12
The Gypsy 13
Dot 15
The Call 16
The Porch 17
Focus 18
Bratenella 19
Very Subtle 20
The Wizard 21
Lady of the Universe 22
Just a Thought 23
Good-Will 24
Rage 26
Turning Leaves 28
Color Me Beautiful 29
Reality 30
How do I love Thee? 32
Empowerment 33
Full Bloom 34
Grains of Sand 35

Out of the Box	36
Freedom	37
Friends	38
Cherish	39
My Nicest Thoughts	40
Believe	41
Reflect	42
Take Time to Bark at the Moon	43
Magic	44
Nana	45
Reflection	46
Courage of the Artist	47
A Conversation With Myself	48
Yesterday	49
Hello Me	50
Shadow	51
To Meditate	52
Indigo	53
Care free	54
Bill Collector	55
Carmine and the White Gardenias	58
Melody	63
Tell Me What I'm Thinking	66

These poems are dedicated to all the bunnies, bears and unicorns that have touched my life. Any resemblance to the human race is strictly a coincidence.

Norma Jean

A Collection of Poetry and 3 Wicked Excellent Short Stories

Raindrops

I love the rain

There is something about the rain That makes me creative

I love everything about it The sound, the smell
I like to watch it Through my window
I like to go to the beach when it rains And walk in it

Rain is not something we all agree on But it is something we have in common

I wonder what God was thinking When He created rain
Did He say "Today I'm going to create
A miracle that will make people slow down? They Will take their time driving and bundle up so they. Don't get sick. Share a cup of coffee with a Friend and talk about childhood."

And then when the rain stops, God creates a rainbow Or a double rainbow.

So people will actually stop and say "Wow, incredible!"

And for one brief moment, whether they realize it Or not they have witnessed a miracle.

Think Again

Something bothered me the other day. A friend said he had difficulty at work And he would just

Have to change.

This really touched my heart. My reply was to always

Stay who you are. Ignore the arrogance. Continue to do

What you do best.

When you step out the door, Leave it all behind.

Channel into the creative sky. Stop and think

The workforce can be

Like another planet

And it will probably stay that way for centuries. In the meantime, Never change

Because you are a conscientious, considerate person With a remarkable spirit side

And that's what makes some people

Stand apart from others

And continues to put magic back into our lives And this is why I believe in you.

Earth Realm

It is our goal
To learn to get through this We need to choose
Not to be in pain

        Acknowledge and release
        Acknowledge and release
        Acknowledge and release
        Acknowledge and release
        Acknowledge and release
        Acknowledge and release
        Acknowledge and release

        Acknowledge

        And

        Release.

Imagine

Imagine that people respected one another
Regardless of race or religion

That we are not afraid to Speak up for what we believe in With good intention

That each and every artist Puts forth the effort
To share their gifts with confidence
That people not only take time
For the gym, But to meditate as well.

That people will correspond With a greeting card Rather than the latest technology

That people will respect Mother Earth and the environment And take enough time to recognize The indigo sky and the harvest moon, The trees, the air that we breathe, The soil or sand beneath our feet

That the brilliant minds of Conventional and holistic medicine Work together to find better cures

That you believe in the Universe So the Universe will believe in you

The Gypsy

Someone once said to me,
My gypsy lifestyle had taken a toll on my friends,
That knowing her, gave me credibility to get on my feet.

I soon realized that I could never be a part of her Life.
Nor could she be a part of mine.

I then realized that I love being a gypsy.

Love like a gypsy,
dance like a gypsy,
Smile like a gypsy,
God loves a gypsy!

Dot

Hi -- My name is Dot.

Hello Dot.
Dot, would you like to be my friend?
Hello Dot, would you like to go shopping?

Oh no, I don't want to shop.
I want to pay bills to buy a house.

Let me show you how.
First you clean up your credit
And when you do
You will not have any credit.

And then you cannot buy a house
Because you need a bill.
You need a bill because
You have to show integrity

And a good payment history.
Sort of like a habitual liar.
then your credit score won't change Because you won't have a bill
And you don't want a bill.

So sorry Dot, but you cannot buy a house.
Now do you want to go shopping Dot?

The Call

The call.
The call.
It's Mom. It's time.
I need you to come.
With a steady, soft whisper she lets me know.
The cancer is back. She has no fear in her voice.
Just a matter-of-fact. "It's time."

Time.
I say I'm ready, but I'm not.
I know that in a short time
I will have to allow her to slip
On to her next journey.
Like her father – my grandfather –
She will probably die in my arms.
I will no longer be able to call her
Every day, just to share goofy stories.
I must let her go.

No one else will ever understand me
Or love me unconditionally.
No one else will say it's okay
When its not.
All I can do is love her,
Try to be as strong as she always has been, Walk to my own tune
And always hold my head up high
Just like mom.

The Porch

*When most people think of a gallery
They think of pristine shops with perfect
Frames and mats and a very quiet,
Subdued atmosphere.*

*However, my version is kind of like a home.
It is busy, with corners filled to the brim
And treasures galore.*

*The gallery is not only a creation of art
But a celebration of life.
As it should be.*

Focus

Perhaps when life is difficult
What we really need to do
Is put some magic back in the day
And see the whole thing through.

Appreciate the beauty in this place we
Call Earth.
Count your blessings, not your woes,
Give meaning to your birth.

Create a place called "Happiness"
And you will have a better day,
Capture the beauty about you,
Until you find your way.

Bratenella

I am a brat
Because I want to be.

I like being a brat

And I know how to spell
B-R-A-T.

So I can be a brat.
And I am a brat.
And I enjoy being a brat.

It takes a lot out of a girl
To be a brat.

But this is my contribution to the world.

Thank you

Sincerely

BRAT

PS - I am never bored.

Very Subtle

Try to look at life

Through the eyes of a true artist

Seeing beauty and definition

To all that exists

Not with arrogance or attitude

But a humbleness

Recognizing that all

Life forms have a purpose

The Wizard

I sat on the corner of the sidewalk
The tears welled in my eyes
I was cold,
Humiliated, despondent and confused.

I asked God why
And I raised my chin
And opened my eyes,
And I saw a wizard.

He extended his hand
And said
"I am the seeker of integrity and compassion. My goal is to create balance and harmony And a better understanding of the universe. From this moment on you will never walk alone."

When they say that God never deserts us, They are simply speaking the truth.

Lady of the Universe

This beautiful Goddess
    The one that reminds you
        Of Infinite possibilities
        Of manifesting with good intentions
        Of the opportunity to share
Enlightenment
        The power of support
        The experience that life gives allows A better
understanding of the entire universe
        For this we are eternally grateful

Just a Thought

Live life with good intention
And passion
Create a space that is comfortable
Take time to meditate
Reflect on blessings
On any circumstance, situation
Or place that you might be
Take time to rest
Sleep is necessary
And very healing

Good-Will

When people ask me why
I create my own jobs,
I tell them that I am
unfit for the workforce!
For those of us unfit for the workforce
I bring you good will

I am the boss—B-O-S-S
I have been here since
     before the building was placed.
I will smile at you,
     then stab you in the back.
I will tell you when to speak
     and when to shut up –

Because I am the boss and I was here first.

I will say "You did a great job,"
     then set you up,
Because I am the boss
     and no job is good enough.

*I will yell and embarrass you in front of customers,
Because I am the boss
  and I know everything,
    and because I was here first.*

*Sometimes there are two bosses,
  one in the morning
    and one at night
      and on weekends.*

*We both terrorize you
because although we smile at each other,
  we really hate each other,
    and take it out on you.*

*Kind of like two male dogs in a pissing match
  and, of course, we're bosses.
    But that is another poem.*

And boss is a four-letter word.

Rage

Well
it's time to
          kick ass
          get drunk
          get high
Mud wrestling
a few barroom brawls
would be nice.

'Bout now
I would like
          a few more belts of bourbon
          couple downers
          some hard rock or
          heavy metal crankin' on the stereo.

Yeah,
that would be nice
but I think I better
          take the cookies out of the oven,
          pickup the kids from school,
          put dinner on
          greet my husband at the door,
          do the dishes,
          take a hot bubble bath
and go to bed.

Dear John-Joe-Fred-Jack-Arnie or whoever you are:

So.
You stood me up.
Oh, yes. I understand.
The kids were sick.
You didn't have your cell phone.

Well,
Being the strong,
Independent
Semi-radical
New-age
Woman that I am,
I did not sit by the phone
And wolf down boxes of bon-bons.
I didn't give you a second, third or fourth thought.
Instead, I ran around the block several times,
Did seventy-thousand jumping jacks
Painted an intricate mantra on the ceiling
Smudged the house
And went to bed.

Affectionately yours.

Kiss my arse.

Turning Leaves

Life is like a good book
As we turn each page we
Encounter a new adventure
Each paragraph sparks
A moment of excitement so –
Wouldn't it be fair to say
each day we encounter is a page-turner?

In spite of the fact that we live in the moment,
Each step is a step toward our future
Every second of the way.
Occasionally we turn back the pages and relive them
And sometimes we skip a few a pages – maybe
To look at the pictures.

Could that be manifesting into the next chapter of our lives
Or could it just be letting the pages turn into leaves
Floating off the trees in a gentle cycle of wind
To simply embrace our journey.

Color Me Beautiful

The beauty of our earth is breath taking
And if you incorporate the nature around us
With pure love
It is a magical combination.
Respect Mother Earth

And Color Me Beautiful

Reality

Come little lady, apply for this card And we'll give you extra miles and a t-shirt.

I'm so sorry.
According to your credit history
We cannot approve you at this time.
But we will bombard you with junk mail.

We may continue to deny you
Or we will give you
An unbelievable credit interest hike
So that when you pay your utilities,
Buy the kids clothes
And feed them,
Remember the grocery store
Does accept cards.

We can continue to keep you in debt
So you can feel like you're
Drowning in deep shit.

This will continue
Until you become somber and despondent,
Until your spirit side kicks in.

Sorry, you are not qualified for this job.
Sorry, you are over qualified for this job.
Maybe you are a corporate spy and want my job.
Sorry, we can't pay you enough to work here,
But will you work here anyway?

Mommy, I need new clothes.
Mommy, Mommy — hey, Mommies don't cry.

How do I love Thee?

You said marry me…
Was it marry me for your green card
Or was it marry me so I can
Do the dishes
Clean the house
Have wild, spontaneous sex
Was it marry me – you need
A tax write-off
Or was it marry me – you
Respect me
My space
I'm fun even when I pout
You like my energy

So it's marry me
Or don't marry me
Just grow old with me
Because I really, truly love you.

Empowerment

How can we be so strong and independent? This is the example that women set before us.

It is better to be soft and sweet than mean. If someone hurts you, can you give it to the Universe and send them on their way In Love and Light?

If someone ridicules you and challenges you,
Let them have the last word and realize that they
Believe they are right.

The Lord says walk in the light
as you see the light.

Try not to judge.

Confide in your dearest confidante.

Walk in the path of love
And cherish every waking moment.

Full Bloom

Since it is spring
Everything is in
     full bloom
Let's kick life into
     full bloom
Like celebrate
Create contrast
Life is short and delicate
And from this very moment
Look at life in
     full bloom.
If life starts to get your down
Swing into
     full bloom
Not hectic is
     full bloom
Seize the day
Because I wish you
     full bloom

Grains of Sand

The other day I went for a walk on the beach

The sun gently warmed the ocean as the
Waves caressed the rocks
With a shimmering spray of silver
From the blue ocean

The beach was littered with driftwood
But it just seemed so natural

As I stood in the sand
And gazed past the horizon
I appreciated the serenity and solitude

The natural beauty

The earth was so alive with energy

I was ever so grateful

Out of the Box

As we get older, things change.
Things that are important
A few years back
Have taken a back seat
To things that really matter.

Most people age with integrity and dignity
Like a fine bottle of wine.

And others sour and grow bitter with time.

We each take so many different roads.

    Some of us capture the essence of the road,
        The air that we breathe,
        The dirt at our feet,
        The gentle breeze against our skin,
        The magic and beauty of the land
        That surrounds us.

We don't have to walk in high social circles
To grasp life.
You don't have to have tons of toys and stuff
        To connect with the universe.
But you do have to step

Out
    Of
        The
            Box.

Freedom

Born to a legacy
Of pride, beauty and culture,
The old soul in a
Young woman's body.

Her eyes could bore a hole
Right to the core of your heart.
She could waltz into
Any room or situation
With a proud independence
That would captivate her audience
In a New York Minute.

She graced the table
With a laced drape,
Lit a candle and
A leaf of sage,
And artistically spread
Her tarot cards.

She scanned the room.
As each client stepped forward
She spoke the truth
Of their deepest secrets, desires and dreams.

Friends

We had been friends a long time.
    After visits we always embraced.
        At one point in time we hugged,

          And as I pulled away
He gently pulled me back into his arms,
    Ran his fingers along my chin,

      and sweetly kissed me on the lips.

It was the most genuine kiss I have ever felt.
      And at that very moment,

   Time stood still.

Cherish

To share my youth
My innermost thoughts
My feelings
My joy
My tears
My triumphs
My tragedy,
Only with you

You are in my thoughts and dreams.
If I could just reach into the heavens
And hold your hand once again!
But instead, I cherish the tender
Memory and sweet embrace of our past
For I had the greatest gift of all by
Knowing your loving spirit and
Togetherness that we shared,
And so, I have learned not to take life
For granted.

But to live each day to its fullest and cherish
Every moment.

My Nicest Thoughts

I think of riding a unicorn
On sandy shores across the ocean
And off above the sunset
Into rainbows and stars
But only with you.

I cherish the thoughts of
Making love near giant redwoods
Under the sun peeking through
Just a hint of light, deep in to the forest,
With you.

Your warmth – your beauty,
Has filled my world with love,
I've shared the joy and sincerity
Hidden deep in your heart.
I've shared with you all my inner fears,
All my inner thoughts
And you've softened them for
I no longer have fear, only thoughts of joy and love,
For the time and for the thoughts that were shared,
Your mind has listened, your thoughts sometimes spoken,
Sometimes seen in your eyes.
Your arms have held me through the worst and through
The best of times.

Yes, my nicest thoughts are
Riding far off, close in your arms
Near the love that I cherish –
My nicest thoughts are of you.

Believe

Life can be a celebration
Of love, joy, laughter
And great happiness.

It is a time of sharing,
Creating, of setting
Examples for our children.

To recognize both our blessings
And just how very special
Each and every one of us can be.

Reflect

*I no longer dread and whine
about our past.
Gone are the dark shadows
That used to hang over me every time
I remember the painful words or
Unjust thoughts
And actions upon us that become part
of your daily routine.*

*When someone says "I love you,"
I say, "I love me too."*

Take Time to Bark at the Moon

Pay attention to the
    Full Moon
The energy and substance of the
    Full Moon
Has quite an effect on its creatures.

Take advantage of the
    Full Moon
        to be
Creative
    Enlightened
        And to bring forth
Recognition
    And gratitude to
        Mother Nature

Magic

Each of us are here for a reason,
And even though we must dance to our own tune, I would ask that we walk the path of integrity.

Dare to be different.
Make strong statements with actions,
Not words.
Have respect for all living creatures.
And compassion.
Take on each endeavor
With the joy of a happy child.

Never mistake kindness for weakness,
And never be afraid to walk the path alone.

For in truth, if you believe in the universe,
You are never alone.

Nana

Will you be there to pick me up,
If I start to fall?

When I am weak and you are
Strong, will you care at all?

If I lose my temper, will you
Know what to do?

Will you have the strength and love
Just to see me through?

If I forget where things have been,
Just what will you say?

Could you help me remember,
Could we make it through the day?

I'll be there to see you through, in every step you take.

I'll walk with you, I'll cherish you, with every change you make.
I'll be there to comfort you, just as you did for me.
Because I was once a little girl and I can clearly see.
You were there to pick me up if and when I fell.
You were strong when I was sick and the doctor came to call.

You always had an answer and you knew just what to do.
You were always there for me and I'll be there for you.

Norma Jean

Reflection

At this very moment
The high mountains
Are full of snow

The clouds are
Kissing the horizon
With a bit of sun
Peeking through

There are shadows
Of electric light
In hues of the brightest white
And a neon blue

They are surrounded
By a variety of pine trees
I am witnessing God's creation
A work of art at its finest

I am grateful to appreciate it.
    Such beauty gives me inner strength
    It allows me to focus
    To the center of my soul
    And allows my spirit energy to cleanse
    It awakens the artist in me
    And makes me rethink what is
    Most important in life.

Courage of the Artist

Some of us live under bridges

And some of us live in the house

On the highest part of the hill

But we all have one thing in common

Our canvas, our board, our rock

That we paint on or use to create

Is our statement

And it continues to speak long after

The paint has worn and the clay has chipped away

You see, one thing that all artists share

Is that we speak through our art

And our art speaks through eternity

Long after we're gone

A Conversation With Myself

*It took me 30 seconds
To get over you –
Is that rude?*

*No, it's just reality setting in.
It's a jump start into the future.
It's a walk on the wild side.
It's taking time to reach for the stars,
And to cherish
The dirt in my garden.*

*It's the quiet in the morning
That I so dearly love.
It's the leaves falling off the trees.
It's that second cup of coffee
Before my bubble bath.
It's counting my blessings,
Not my woes.*

*But I need to ask myself:
Was it getting over you?
Or getting over me*

Yesterday

Seems like yesterday
As I stepped out of the car
And felt the warm embrace of the sun
I saw shadows of light
And heard conquering ocean waves
The cries of the gull
The smell of coffee from the local diner
And the laughter of the early morning clients
Fishermen walking across the yards
To make things work
The heartbeat of a harbor
Pulse
It seems like yesterday
But it's still alive in my heart

Hello Me

Today give yourself
The gift of happiness
Of expression with
Good intention
Create something beautiful
Think abundance
As spiritual and not material
And be okay with who you are

Shadow

I love the night
When the stars meet the moon
And the air still has a chill
When the indigo sky casts shadows
And the beauty of Mother Earth
Speaks to all who will listen
When the soft whisper of the wind
Sends messages to only those
Who will recognize and cherish
The universe.

To Meditate

Stand firmly on the ground
And sink your feet into the earth
Imagine the roots of a tree
Grounding you for balance
Send light energy through your body
Imagine yourself full of love
And good intention

Look to the North and say
Thank you to Mother Earth

Look to the East and
Ask for Abundance

Look to the West and
Send positive thoughts

Look to the South and
Be grateful

North, East, West and South
It spells news
If you practice this daily
It will enhance your life
And others that cross your journey

Indigo

There is something to be said
For the integrity of the earth

Each person must walk to their own tune
And not be too influenced by another human being

Shower your thoughts with good intention
Do not allow anyone to compromise your integrity

Be passionate and profound in your affirmations
Have compassion and present yourself well

But be real

There is always hope and prosperity If you allow it to manifest into your life

Care free

Stress Free
I love the morning when the birds
start to bloom
and the flowers start to sing.

When I wake up to a crisp chill
in the air.
Like the day before the first snow
falls.

I slip my socks on my ears and
my mittens on my feet
and set out

to seize the day.

Bill Collector

#1 you need to be a parasite. You need to have the ability to be cruel, uncaring, bold & insulting. You need to collect that almighty dollar regardless of any hardship from the clients; insult them, threaten them, make them feel small and like a deadbeat no matter what the situation. Tell them how many times they have been late or deferred; make them feel worthless; remember you are the parasite. Suck every ounce of integrity out of this person, and we will give you a commission every time you collect. But if you take their possessions, you will have to go home, look in the mirror and hope that no one is as cruel, humiliating & uncaring to you or anyone close to you, as you have been to your fellow man. Be careful when you are out of the office, you may meet people that show compassion and random acts of kindness, this totally against our policy. For in the walls of our building we crossbreed rats & snakes and clone them into people that become parasites like bill collectors. If you can't cut it, we will pursue a supervisor that could be more cruel & uncaring than you ever imagined. Carry on and remember you get a special bonus for every person and family you destroy.

APPLY WITHIN

I hope you have enjoyed this collection of thoughts. They're a little bit different, I know but then again, so am I. If I have learned anything in life, it is to follow your dreams to believe in every grain of sand, every star and every element of the universe because if you believe then all things are possible Love & Light

~ Norma Jean

3 Wicked, Excellent

Short Stories

By
Norma Jean Campanaro

Carmine and the White Gardenias

I will never mistreat a woman again. She never spoke of any family... little did I know the only family she had were spending 40 to life in one of the most notorious federal prisons of all time...

Every morning we met for coffee at a little diner in downtown New York. There were four of us; Joe, recently retired from the NYPD, Manny, a plumber, Mica, who worked in construction, and me. I'm Carmine. I'm no one special, I just do odd jobs here and there, but I always get by.

There she goes, Anna Maria, every morning buzzing by to those fancy offices down the street; kind of homely for an Italian girl.

The guys started razzing me about asking her out. After a few weeks it got me to thinking. I was walking home from the diner and saw Freddy with his flower cart.

"Hey Carmine, how ya doin'?" "Hey Freddy, what's up?"

"Some stuff, not much news. Steady with little jobs. You know, the usual."

"Hey Freddy! Gimme one of those roses."

"Just one, Carmine? Don't be cheap! Girls don't like cheap, ya know."

I grabbed the rose and snarled at Freddy with a muffled curse. Then as I walked across the street I heard Freddy yelling "Don't be cheap, Carmine!"

The next morning I waited outside the diner, and when Anna Maria came around the corner, I stepped out with the rose. I guess I must have startled her as Anna Maria dropped the file of papers she was carrying, and looked really annoyed. I helped her pick them up as she glared at me. "Sorry about that," I mumbled. "Anyway, what's a pretty girl like you doing with all this work?"

She glanced up at me, and I thought to myself "ok, here it goes." "Maybe some time I could buy you some coffee. You know, to sort of make up for scaring you. I'm sorry. Oh, here. Have a rose." I gave it to her and kept scooping up papers and feeling really stupid when she didn't say anything.

All of a sudden she scribbled on a card and handed it to me, "Thursday, 7 P.M. sharp. My place. Don't be late."

My head was spinning as she took off. It was Tuesday. I didn't want to say anything to the guys.

Thursday rolls around and I go over to Anna Maria's neighborhood. I sniff the air and think "wow, someone's cooking something around here." I find her house and the source of the tempting smells. We spend the evening eating great food, drinking great wine, and end up in bed having great sex too.

I wake up in the morning to the smell of fresh coffee and my head still spinning from the wine the night before. Anna Maria was up early cooking breakfast. I take a hot shower and walked back into the bedroom at the same time as Anna Maria was bringing me a tray filled with breakfast. It all seemed a little surreal to me. I wasn't used to this happening so fast.

We talked for a while, and I offered to help with odd jobs around the house. Without hesitation Anna Maria mentioned that she could use some help with some remodeling she wanted done. Without much thought we agreed that I would move in and manage the upgrade and upkeep of the house.

After Anna Maria left for work, I headed over to the diner to tell the guys. I went on and on about how great the set up was with the good food and the great sex. The guys didn't seem so thrilled, but I tuned them out, "You guys think too hard. Don't worry; I'm not in it for the long haul."

I started to get into the routine of the remodeling work, replacing pipes and floors and so on. Anna Maria never said much about my choices in color or wood or carpet. Instead she seemed pleased with the work I was doing. I laughed as I shared my stories with the guys.

"Some shmuck sends her white gardenias and doesn't even send a card. I take them and make her think they're from me," I laughed. The guys just listened and stared at me.

Around six or seven months later I was full on into the remodel. There wasn't all that much left to work on. Mornings at the diner have become far and few between. There was one room which I never worked on – Anna Maria's office. I just never paid much attention to it. But as I had nothing better left to do, I went in.

As I opened the door and stepped into the office, I spotted a row of shelves against one of the walls. They looked a little shakey to me, so I decided to start there. As I started removing the shelves and questioning the support system and mumbling to myself about the shoddy work, the whole thing came down along with a piece of the wall paneling. But it just got worse from there.

Behind the wall panel was more cash than I had seen in my lifetime. I felt sick to my stomach. I knew it was too good to be true. She had a double life. Oh, this is bad. I glanced at the clock. I have to get this put back together. I tried to get it back to where I remembered everything to be, and I tried to act normal when Anna Maria got home that evening. But I couldn't sleep and tossed and turned all night.

After Anna Maria left for work the next morning, I booked it over to the diner.

"Hey Carmine! Where have you been?" The guys were glad to see me. After a little small talk, Joe pulled me aside.

"Carmine, are you okay?"

"Yeah, yeah. I'm fine, Joe. Why?" I asked.

"Well, some guys were looking for you. Tough guys. You're not gambling again, are you, Carmine?" "No, Joe. Everything is okay. I promise." Joe really looked concerned.

After coffee, I went for a walk to try and decide what to do. I didn't want to go back to Anna Maria. I still had a loft above the junkyard I could live at. I turned down an alley as a short cut to go back and get my stuff before she got home. As I got halfway down, I saw a dark town car with tinted windows pull into the alley, blocking the exit. I turned and saw another pulling in behind me.

Six months later…

The state inspector spoke to the gentleman at the nursing home. "I'm always so impressed by your facility. The state made a good choice funding this program. A men's home run by all male staff. Spotless with white marble columns, men in scrubs with white gardenias pinned to *the collars..." Her thoughts were interrupted by sobs from a man in a wheel chair.*

As a staff member turned to console him, the man in charge explained. "Poor soul. They found him in an alley. Said his hair turned white literally overnight. He can't communicate, and we can't identify him."

"That's a shame," the inspector replied.

The men escorted the state inspector to the door. As she exited, she noticed that the walkway was lined with white gardenias. Their fragrance was a little overwhelming. As she walked down the path, she couldn't shake the edgy feeling she got when recalling the man in the wheelchair. She could still hear his sobbing as she walked away.

Oh, what tangled webs we weave.

Melody

Melody the artist. Once as vibrant and full of life as her name – until she fell in love...

The hospital administrator, the supervisor of nurses, and the licensed tech stood at the large window overlooking a client in a wheelchair on a beautifully manicured lawn in front of a large oak tree.

"Jonathan, it's not healthy for you to be so invested with this client. There is no hope. She's going to be placed in a home tomorrow afternoon."

"But I know I can reach her. I just know I can. Give me a chance!

Just another 48 hours!"

The administrator and nurse looked discretely at each other and shook their heads. The administrator took a step back and said, "48 hours and that's all." Jonathan, with a sigh of relief, sprinted out to the walkway and across the lawn.

"Melody," he called in a soft voice, "I know you can hear me. Please, they are going to place you in a home if you don't respond." Melody sat with a blank stare., shoulders rolled almost motionless.

Melody at one time was as vibrant and lively as her name. An artist so full of life and vivid bright color until she made a mistake – she fell deeply in love.

Jonathan continued to plead with her until he stood up and spoke in a soft breath, "forget this. There's no use." Feeling defeated he started to walk away. With a bout of energy, Melody spoke, "wait."

Jonathan looked stunned and stared at Melody in disbelief.

"I hear you, Melody," he replied. And for the next 2 ½ hours she told her story.

"I met him at my art shows. He came to every one of them. It wasn't until the 3rd show that we actually spoke. He wasn't really my type, but the guy I was dating was totally self-destructive and I knew the relationship would go nowhere.

"I see women come through here all the time. I record it all in my head. Everything. The same old thing over and over. They come in crying and beaten down, all in the name of love.

"We spoke of abstract art. He had a strange concept of art, a little intriguing at times. I guess I was just curious about him. The first year was ok. The 2nd year I didn't know whether to get off the couch in the morning and make coffee or kill myself. Nothing was ever good enough, quick enough, the right color, the right size, until nothing even mattered. It started to affect my art, and I just couldn't cope anymore.

"That's when you guys found me and took me away."
Jonathan was writing and recording everything in avid detail. He wheeled Melody back to her room and reported to the administrator and staff. The very next day they set a room for Melody to paint. Each day Melody would retreat to the room and within a short time would complete the painting. She would paint from morning to late evening, and if not reminded she would forget to stop to eat.

Each evening she methodically placed her brushes in a semi-circle according to size. The staff was amazed at her paintings and her progress. Sometimes visitors would mistake Melody for a hospital employee. Each shift was eager to check out the progress of her painting. It became part of the daily routine. The paintings were absolutely beautiful. One evening, Melody worked rather late on a large painting.

The night nurse checked in and reminded her, "not too late tonight, Melody. We're short of staff."

"See you in the morning." "Good night, dear"

The next morning, still short of staff, and with people coming and going, no one noticed the pretty young woman by the garden door. Everyone was interrupted by a scream from Melody's room. The night staff was asleep in his chair, and Melody was nowhere to be found. The Head of Nursing was viewing each painting while everyone was frantically searching for Melody.
The Head of Nursing stood and stared at the last completed painting. "She's gone."

"She's not gone," argued one of the nurses. "She's just hiding."

The Head of Nursing pointed to the paintings. Each one revealed the path that Melody had lived. A lovely young artist sitting by a gallery wall full of vibrancy and laughter. A polished young lady stepping into the open house, arm entwined with a man with no facial features. An abstract that looked like a hurricane. And last of all, an angel walking across the hospital lawn under an oak tree into the sunrise when it is said angels walk among us.

"I do believe that this is true, and I do believe that Melody chose to be one of those angels."

Tell Me What I'm Thinking

My name is Mia. I was named after my mother who was named after my grandmother. We have a long legacy of secrets all documented for centuries in an ornate copper box.

Not to be shared, not for the weak of heart.

Soaking in my bubble bath surrounded by candles, I drift off to thoughts in my dream state of a dark town car and handsome, yet evil man only to be rudely jolted awake by my neighbor banging on my garden door.

"Hello?"

"Hello, Mia! It's me, Ms. Emily."

"Hello, Ms. Emily!" I slip on my robe and shuffle toward the door. "What can I do for you?" I shoo my cat as he hisses at her.

"Oh, that kitty of yours!" she replies in a soft voice. "Did you make a gentleman out of him yet?" Rambling on about a neighborhood rummage sale, her mouth drops.

Oh, the box. Why didn't I put it away?

"Oh, that lovely box! Heard it's been in your family for years. When will you let me peek?"

"I really need..." I started to say."

"Oh of course, dear! You'll catch a cold in this drafty home!" She hands me a flyer, glares at my cat and chooses to leave.

It is a drafty house, yet it's been in my family for years. I tuck the box in a special place where it is securely kept. Off to work. It's a bit of a hike to station 206. 2 0 6 = 8, a money number. On bus 3, a master number. To a reading room surrounded by magnificent gardens.

I set up my table, candle, and stone of the day. One of the girls calls an emergency meeting in the tea room. Everyone is sobbing. Kind of reminds me of when a group of fundamentalists tried to close us down about a year ago. Maya gathers us together. Maya owns the reading room.

"Ladies, you must be very careful. Rita, our sister reader, has been brutally attacked. We don't exactly have a very traditional profession. I sincerely urge you to use extreme caution."

Rita, sweet Rita. I go back to my room, gather my cards and crystals to go to the only hospital in town. Small town living, the desk nurse gave me room number 303 without even looking at me. I step down the hall and peek in lean toward Rita and start to speak softly,

"Sweet, sweet Rita. I am..."

Before I could finish, in a harsh voice, with great effort Rita says, "He wants the box." She crosses to her next journey. The machines go off and I back towards the door. The crash cart is flying down the hall yet I know she is gone.

Each day I travel the same route to the same reading room. Eleven months pass. Eleven Psychics buried in the little cemetery garden near the reading room. After each death I could see him. I would set up my table and a town car would pull up along the highway. I would peer through the large windows. There he was, dark evil arms crossed staring at me until I would acknowledge him. Then he would simply get in his car and leave. Why didn't I tell? I did, but I was the only one that could see him. On the 11th month, I had enough. I glared at him, challenged him, wrapped up my cards, crystals and candles and headed home.

As I walked toward the stairs, the wind picked up. The dark clouds started to roll in. It was cold and damp. I centered myself and entered the old house. Hearing the wind whispering messages; we are with you, protect our secret, be strong, listen to our voices.

I lit a leaf of sage, centered the box under my chair, sat and waited for the forces of good and evil about to rock and shake the earth. I sat and rocked back and forth on the chair. I could feel him, smell him. Who is this person, what connects us?

I continued to hear the voices – Be strong, Mia. Be strong. We are with you.

The old house began to shake. The windows rattled, the cold air permeated through the walls.

Lavender. I smell lavender. It makes me dizzy, so familiar. In a trance state I drift. The wind continues to chant, "Tell me what I'm thinking... Preacher's gone a drinking, Grandma cast a spell & Preacher goes to hell." I start to remember. We used to sit in the lavender field and play a game.

Tell me what I'm thinking. We would telepathically transfer thoughts to one another. We would write it in the sand and say tell me what I'm thinking. His father, the town preacher, a pillar of the community. He chased me home and called me a witch. My grandmother was the only one brave enough to stand up to him. All I remember is the smell of lavender and screams.

After that, I never saw my grandmother again. I rock some more in my chair, the box glowing with light and energy. I can hear thunder and lightning. The sky becomes dark and fierce. I can feel him closer and closer. The forces of good and evil are about to shake the entire planet with determination and pride. I continue to rock, hold my head up high and beckon him forward. Chills go through my entire body as I begin to sing "Tell me what I'm thinkin

Seven Wise Women With Positive Four-Letter Words

Printed by Libri Plureos GmbH in Hamburg, Germany